THE FIRST WITNESS

On Job, grief, and the ones who refused to be silenced

Before there was a word for it, there was Job.

He was a righteous man. Faithful. His family intact. Then, in a span of days that the text does not soften, everything was taken. His children died. His wealth was gone. His health collapsed. He sat in ash, covered in sores, and the people closest to him offered him what people have been offering the grieving ever

since

— explanations.

You must have done something wrong. God is testing you. Accept it. Be patient. There is a reason.

Job refused every one of them.

He did not perform acceptance. He did not dress his grief in language that would make the people around him more comfortable. He demanded to be heard — not consoled, not corrected, not managed. Heard. He argued with God directly. He insisted that his experience was real, that his suffering was unjust, and that the silence he was being handed in return was not an answer.

And God, when he finally spoke, said this: Job spoke rightly. The friends with the tidy theological explanations were wrong.

The one who told the truth about what he was carrying was vindicated.

I think about Job often.

Not because my story mirrors his exactly — though there are mornings when the ash feels familiar. I think about him because he was the first witness. The first one to say: this happened, I am not going to explain it away, and I am still here.

That is what a witness does. Not perform recovery. Not arrive at peace on a schedule that makes others comfortable. A witness stays present to what is true, names it accurately, and refuses to let it be erased.

There are 18.7 million bereaved parents in the United States. Most of them have been handed the same thing Job was handed — explanations, platitudes, and a quiet pressure to move on. Most of them have been told, in one way or another, that their grief is a problem to be solved rather than a truth to be witnessed.

Job was not a problem. He was a testimony.

So are they. So are you.

The Book of Job is not a story about suffering ending. It is a story about someone who refused to let suffering be the last word.

Who held his integrity through the silence. Who kept the record even when no one was listening.

That is the oldest field manual I know of for what we carry.

And it begins the same way every testimony begins.

With someone who said:

I was here.

This happened.

Now you know.

— *The Witness · The Echoes Project · 2026*

ANANTA

The Vilomah Chronicle

David Wittenburg

The Echoes Project

The Echoes Project

thewitnessechoes.com

anantavilomah.com

First Edition, 2026

ISBN: 979-8-9956139-6-1

Library of Congress Control Number:
2026912546

The Ananta Framework is documented in
the academic record.

SSRN:6761738
The Permanent Record: anantavilomah.com

MEDICAL AND MENTAL HEALTH WARNING

This book addresses profound grief, child loss, and the permanent psychological state of bereaved parents. The content may be emotionally intense. This book is not a substitute for professional mental health care, therapy, or crisis intervention.

If you are in crisis or experiencing thoughts of self-harm, please contact the 988 Suicide and Crisis Lifeline by calling or texting 988, or text HOME to 741741 (Crisis Text Line). Help is available 24 hours a day, 7 days a week.

The Ananta framework described in this book is a personal and forensic record — not a clinical treatment, diagnosis, or therapeutic model. Readers are encouraged to seek qualified professional support as needed.

For Keith Allen Richards. 1963–1968.

For Jon David Wittenburg. 1994–2015.

For Lauren Elizabeth Wittenburg. 1992–2020.

The graphite is permanent.

The pencil has no eraser.

TABLE OF CONTENTS

FROM THE AUTHOR

I did not write this book to make you comfortable.

I wrote it because 18.7 million people in the United States are walking in their memories of who their children are — present tense, always — and the world built no room for them to say that out loud.

Ananta is that room.

It is the word I found in Sanskrit when the English language failed me for the last time. Infinite. Without end. The precise, forensic description of what it means to carry this baseline for the rest of a life — on good days and bad days and every ordinary Tuesday morning in between.

Conventional therapy was not built for this. It was built around resolution. The Vilomah condition does not resolve. It is
carried consciously, permanently, as truth.

They never go anywhere. That is what is
actually good about Ananta. It is a blessing.

If you are Vilomah — this book was written for you. Not to fix you. Not to move you through stages. To witness you. To say — you are counted. The record is permanent. You are exactly where you are supposed to be.

Vilomah in Ananta.

— *David Wittenburg, The Witness*

The Echoes Project · 2026

PREFACE

Vilomah in Ananta

I feel guilty at times that I am still here.

I will say that plainly because no one else does. The world does not build room for that sentence. The clinical framework has no stage for it. The Grief Industry would prefer you move past it as quickly as possible because guilt is not a destination and the industry runs on destinations.

But it is true. And the truth deserves a witness.

I am still here. Keith is not. Jon is not. Lauren is not.

And I am walking. Not in their memories — in my memories of them. That is a distinction that took years to understand and I am not sure I can fully explain it except to say this: they are not ghosts I am chasing. They are people I loved and love still, held in the only place I have access to — my own recollection of who they are.

Present.

Lauren 9.14 ounces. Two teeth. A head full of hair.

Jon All boy. Quiet. But always there.

Those are my memories. That is what I have. And on the days when life is moving and the weight recedes and I forget for a moment — and then remember that I forgot — the guilt arrives not as dysfunction but as love. As the proof that they were real. That the record is permanent.

Here is what I have learned that no conventional therapy can teach you.

You cannot fight the Ananta state. The more you fight it, the more it reveals itself as the truth you were trying to outrun. It does not respond to stages. It does not respond to timelines. It does not respond to the clinical assumption that resolution is the destination.

I am exactly where I am supposed to be.

Vilomah in Ananta.

Against the natural order. Infinite, without end. Both truths at once, held without apology, carried consciously on good days and bad days and every ordinary day in between.

The Grief Industry wants you to get to a place and stay there. A functional baseline. A managed state. A person who has successfully processed and returned to ordinary life.

I say — you cannot touch me the way God has.

Not through them. Not through their system. Not through their stages or their frameworks or their clinical distance.

Through the tribe. Through the faith. Through the record.

Bob said it simply: You will be better for it.

Not healed. Not resolved. Not graduated from the curriculum of catastrophic loss.

Better. Present. Conscious. Exactly here.

Vilomah in Ananta.

That is where this book begins. That is where it ends. And that is where every one of the 18.7 million who are reading this right now already lives — whether they have the words for it yet or not.

Now you have the words.

Now you know.

— *David Wittenburg, The Witness*

The Echoes Project · 2026

FOREWORD

The Inversion

This is not a book about grief.

The word grief is a soft currency used by a global industry to bridge a gap that cannot be crossed. You misplace your keys. You find your way. A child dies. Those are not the same sentence.

I am The Witness, and I am a Vilomah. This term identifies me as a parent who has outlived their children — an inversion of the natural order that the clinical world often fails to name.

For the 18.7 million in the United States and the billions globally who exist within this wreckage, there is no recovery. There is only the record. I call this infinite architecture Ananta. It is the permanent, forensic evidence of lives that were, and the void that remains.

This work is the deconstruction of the systems that try to soften the unsoftenable. It is a data-driven audit of a demographic that the Grief Industry prefers to keep in the shadows.

Most importantly, it is the Witness Archive for Keith, Jon, and Lauren.

They died. Their record remains.

Now you know.

CHAPTER 1

The Architecture of Inversion

To understand Ananta, one must first acknowledge the structural collapse of the natural order. In the standard human narrative, the timeline moves forward: the old make way for the young. When a child dies, the timeline does not just stop; it inverts. The floor becomes the ceiling, and the survivor is left standing in the wreckage of a system that no longer has a name for them.

The Grief Industry attempts to solve this inversion with a vocabulary of subtraction.

They speak of what happened as if it were a misplaced object, a void that can be filled with enough time and clinical intervention.

Our children died. We carry the weight of that as a forensic fact.

This is the first law of the Ananta record:

A child died. That is not a loss. That is an inversion.

The 18.7 million parents in the United States who exist in this state are not recovering. We are the architects of a new reality. We are the keepers of the Witness Archives, documenting the reality that the world is too uncomfortable to speak aloud.

For Keith, Jon, and Lauren, the record begins here. Not with a whimper of moving on, but with the cold, hard graphite of the truth.

* * *

For Keith Allen Richards. 1963–1968.

For Jon David Wittenburg. 1994–2015.

For Lauren Elizabeth Wittenburg. 1992–2020.

The graphite is permanent.

The pencil has no eraser.

Now you know.

CHAPTER 2

The Grief Industry — A Forensic Audit

There is a multi-billion dollar infrastructure built on the premise that grief can be managed.

It has stages. It has timelines. It has licensed professionals, clinical frameworks, support groups with folding chairs and bad coffee, and a vocabulary so sanitized it barely touches the walls of the room you are actually standing in.

For the Vilomah, none of it was built for us.

The Grief Industry was constructed around a fundamental assumption — that grief is temporary. That with enough time, enough intervention, enough processing, the survivor returns to a functional baseline. The industry measures success by the degree to which the bereaved person stops being bereaved.

This is not grief support. This is erasure with credentials.

The Ananta record does not move toward recovery. It moves toward truth. And the truth is this: when a child dies, the parent does not need a stage. They need a witness.

The 18.7 million Vilomah in the United States have been handed the following, consistently, across decades of clinical practice — silence dressed up as support. Five stages that were never designed for them. A language of subtraction that turns the weight of a child's death into a problem to be solved.

The problem is not the grief. The problem is the architecture that was never built to hold it.

This is the second law of the Ananta record: *The Grief Industry was not built for the Vilomah. We built our own.*

* * *

For Keith — who died in 1968 before the industry had even finished building its first stage.

For Jon — who died in 2015 while the industry handed out worksheets.

For Lauren — who died in 2020 while the world was too busy to count the ones who were already gone.

The record does not forgive the gap.

It documents it.

Now you know.

CHAPTER 3

The Billion — The Scale of the Unspeakable

Since 1950, approximately 990 million children have died globally.

Not lost. Not passed. Not gone too soon. Died.

One billion children. Seventy-five years. The UN counted them. Our World in Data charted them. UNICEF published the reports. And yet — not one government on earth has built a registry for the parents who outlived them.

In 1950, twenty million children died in a single year. One in four children did not reach age fifteen. By 2024 that number had dropped to under five million annually — a triumph of medicine, nutrition, and infrastructure that the world rightly celebrates.

But no one counted what was left behind.

For every child who died, there was at least one Vilomah created. One parent pushed against the natural order. One person for whom the timeline inverted and never corrected itself.

The mathematics are simple. The silence around them is not.

In the United States alone, 18.7 million parents have outlived a child. Globally the number does not have a ceiling. It has been accumulating since 1950 — through famine, through war, through opioids, through accidents, through the quiet and ordinary catastrophes that do not make headlines.

The Grief Industry counted the stages. Nobody counted us.

This is the third law of the Ananta record:

The scale of the Vilomah has never been fully acknowledged.

The record acknowledges it now.

* * *

For Keith. 1963–1968. Five years. Counted here.

For Jon. 1994–2015. Twenty-one years. Counted here. For Lauren. 1992–2020. Twenty-eight years. Counted here.

The graphite is permanent.

The pencil has no eraser.

Now you know.

CHAPTER 4

The Lineage — Where the Witness Begins

Every Ananta record has a starting point.

The Wittenburg name traces through the American Midwest — Illinois, Missouri, Tennessee — families who came, planted, built, and buried their own. Ordinary American genealogy until it was not.

The 1950 Census captures a moment in time. A country rebuilding after war. Families settling into the postwar architecture of normalcy

— steady jobs, growing children, futures that seemed guaranteed by simple

arithmetic.

In 1961, in Arkansas, one of those families had a son. David.

The blueprint begins there.

Seven years later, in 1968, the first inversion occurred. A brother died. Keith. Four years old. The natural order broke for the first time in that family and nobody had a word for what the parents became. Vilomah was not in the American vocabulary. It still is not.

The 1950 Census counted the Wittenburgs. It did not count what was coming for them.

This is what genealogical records cannot hold — the weight of what happened after the counting stopped. The archives have the names. The addresses. The occupations. What they do not have is the forensic record of the inversions. The deaths. The Vilomah.

That is what Ananta is for.

The record the census never built — this is it.

* * *

For Keith Allen Richards. 1963–1968.

The first name in the Witness Archive.

The first inversion. The one the language had no word for.

The graphite is permanent.

The pencil has no eraser.

Now you know.

CHAPTER 5

Keith — The First Inversion

The blueprint begins on August 28, 1961.

I was born into an Arkansas world that still felt solid. Solid the way only childhood can feel solid — unquestioned, unexamined, simply there. That solidity lasted six years.

In 1967, the geography of my life shifted forever.

I was six years old, sitting in a hospital in Stuttgart, Arkansas, listening to a transistor radio, when the DJ's voice cut through the static.

A young boy, just four years old.

That boy was my brother.

I did not know he had died. I was sitting there — a six-year-old in a hospital, the radio on — and I did not know. I remember him in the back seat of the car, lifeless. I remember the wreck. And then I remember the hospital. And the radio. And the DJ's voice.

And in the background — the wailing of my grandmother.

I did not have a word for that sound. I did not have a word for what she was. I did not have a word for what my family had just become. I only knew that the sound she made was the most honest thing I had ever heard — a sound the body makes when the natural order inverts and the language fails completely.

And then Keith was just gone.

That is the first law of the Ananta record in its rawest form. Not a clinical definition. Not a forensic framework. A six-year-old boy. A transistor radio. A grandmother's wail. And a brother who was there — quiet, sweet-

mannered, always there — and then was not.

He was only given four years to leave a record. Four years before the inversion. Four years before the floor became the ceiling and nobody in that hospital, nobody on that radio, nobody in the English language had a word for what our family had just become.

Vilomah.

The Ananta record does not require volume. It requires truth.

* * *

Keith Allen Richards. 1963–1968. Four years old.

He was quiet. But he was always there.

The graphite is permanent.

The pencil has no eraser.

Now you know.

INTERLUDE

The Space Between

There is no chapter for what happens next.

That is the problem.

The Ananta record holds the account. The events are documented. The record is set. But what the record cannot hold — what no record has ever been built to hold — is the space between the names.

Between Keith and Jon there were forty-seven years.

Forty-seven years of a man who carried the first inversion inside him — quietly, without a word in the English language for what he was — while the world asked him to function. To work. To build. To show up. To be present for other people's ordinary days while the floor underneath him had not been level since Stuttgart, Arkansas, 1968.

Nobody pauses there. Nobody writes about the forty-seven years between the first death and the second. The Grief Industry does not have a stage for it. The clinical framework does not have a name for it. The world does not have the patience for it.

But the Vilomah lives there.

In the space between the names. In the ordinary Tuesday mornings that arrive without warning and sit on your chest like a stone. In the moment you reach for a memory and find only fragments — a back seat, a transistor radio, a grandmother's wail — and realize that the fragments are all you have and they are going to have to be enough.

This is what Ananta is for. Not just the deaths. The space between them.

The forty-seven years between Keith and Jon.

The five years between Jon and Lauren.

The silence that has no name and no stage and no clinical intervention and no end.

The Witness lived there. He is still there.

The record acknowledges it now.

CHAPTER 6

Jon — The Always Wanted

There is a kind of son that every man carries in his mind before the son ever arrives.

Not a fantasy. Not a projection. Just a quiet certainty — that when the time came, when the boy arrived, he would be exactly this. Present. Happy. All boy. The one who carries the name forward. The one who makes the weight of everything that came before worth

carrying.

Jon was that son.

Not because he was perfect. Not because he was without struggle. But because he was genuinely happy. That is rarer than people know. In a world that hands you a list of things to worry about, Jon was not on the list. He was not a concern. He was the one who showed up, all boy, full of the kind of life that makes a father believe the record can be something other than inversion.

He was the always wanted.

Before Jon there was the pattern nobody talked about.

I came from a big family. His mother came from a big family. And somewhere in the middle of building a life together, we noticed something that the world does not have a framework for.

Her brother died. My brother died.

Then our son died.

Three siblings. Two families. One inversion that crossed bloodlines and decades and found us anyway.

Nobody handed us a word for that either.

Nobody sat us down and said — you two were marked before you found each other. That the Vilomah was already in the architecture of both families before Jon ever arrived. Before the always wanted ever took his first breath.

I do not know what to do with that. I am not sure anyone does.

What I know is this — Jon arrived into a family that had already been asked to survive the unsurvivable once on each side. And he was happy. Genuinely, completely happy. Like he did not know the weight of what had come before him. Like he was the answer to all of it.

Maybe he was.

And then on December 6, 2015, a daughter's voice shattered a Sunday morning.

Jon's dead, Dad. Jon's dead.

No warning. No preparation. No order of magnitude. One day here. Next day gone.

Just gone.

That is the second inversion. Not a grief stage. Not a clinical event. The floor becoming the ceiling for the second time in one life — and the world kept moving like it did not happen.

* * *

Jon David Wittenburg.

1994–2015. Twenty-one years old.

The always wanted. The one who carried the name.

He was here. The record says so.

The graphite is permanent.

The pencil has no eraser.

Now you know.

CHAPTER 7

Lauren — The Middle Child

She came in at 9.14 ounces. Two teeth. A head full of hair.

From the very beginning Lauren Elizabeth Wittenburg arrived like she had already figured something out that the rest of us were still working on.

She was the middle child. Need I say more.

Anyone who has ever known a middle child knows the particular genius of it — the watching, the waiting, the quiet calculation. Lauren would observe what her sister did. She would watch the parental reaction. File it. And then — quietly, with that particular Lauren energy that was up to no good and completely aware of it — she would make her move.

She and Jon were thick as thieves.

Two children who found each other inside the same family and decided that was their team. Their frequency. Their room. Jon all boy, Lauren all mischief, both of them alive in the way that only people who are genuinely happy can be alive — completely, fully, without apology.

The Grief Industry will hand you a framework for what happened in 2020. It will give you language and stages and clinical distance.

I am not interested in any of that.

What I am interested in is the 9.14 ounces. The two teeth. The head full of hair. The middle child who watched and waited and was quietly, completely, magnificently up to no good.

That is Lauren. That is the record.

* * *

Lauren Elizabeth Wittenburg.

1992–2020. Twenty-eight years old.

Thick as thieves with Jon.

Always.

The graphite is permanent.

The pencil has no eraser.

Now you know.

CHAPTER 8

The 18.7 Million — The Global Catastrophe Nobody Has Time For

18.7 million.

That is the number of parents in the United States who have outlived a child. Right now. Today. While you are reading this sentence.

Not historical. Not past tense. Right now.

And that is just the United States.

Since 1950, approximately 990 million children have died globally. Nearly one billion children. The UN counted them. Our World in Data charted them. UNICEF published the annual reports. In 1950 alone, twenty million children died in a single year — one in four children never reached age fifteen.

By 2024 that number had dropped to under five million annually.

I am grateful the number came down. From twenty million to under five million — that is medicine, nutrition, and infrastructure.
That is human progress and it deserves acknowledgment.

But here is what nobody says out loud.

You cannot celebrate a number that still bears relevance.

Five million children still dying every year. Still. In 2024. And for every one of those children — a Vilomah is created.

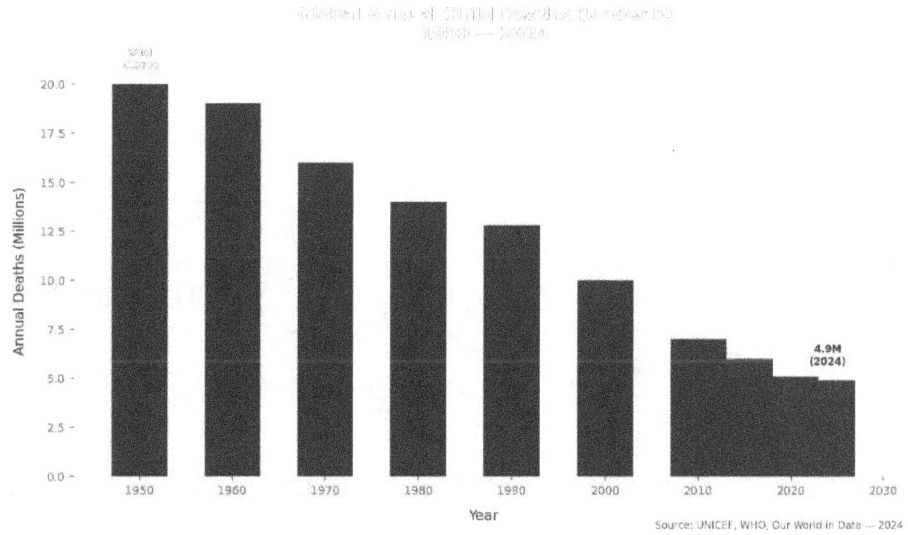

Annual global child deaths under age five, 1950–2024.

Source: UNICEF, WHO, Our World in Data.

The opioid crisis gets a task force. Gun violence gets a commission. Cancer gets a billion dollar research infrastructure.

The Vilomah gets silence.

Not one registry. Not one agency. Not one room. Since 1950.

That is not a gap in the system. That is the system working exactly as designed — which is to say, not for us. Never for us. The Vilomah has always been asked to process privately, grieve quietly, and return to function as quickly as possible so the world can keep moving.

Every hour, approximately 560 to 600 children under the age of five die globally. Expand that to children under fifteen and the figure rises to approximately 685 per hour — 16,440 per day — 6 million per year. Source: UNICEF, WHO, Our World in Data. 2024.

2 out of every 10 people on this planet exist in the Global Wreckage — carrying the Ananta state, walking in their memories of who their child is. Present tense. Always.

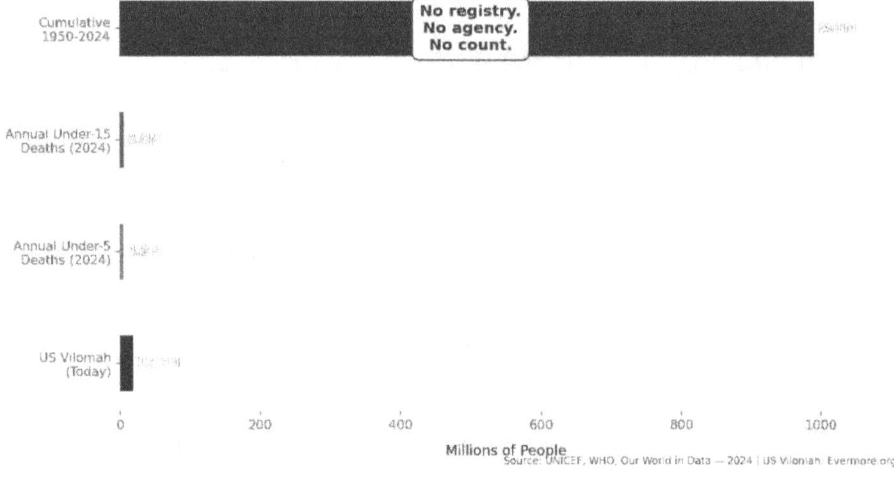

The scale of the Vilomah by the numbers.

Source: UNICEF, WHO, Our World in Data, Evermore.org.

The global mental health infrastructure spends the majority of its resources on what is diagnosable, treatable, and resolvable. According to the WHO, countries spend on average less than 2% of their national health budgets on

mental health. Of that, the majority goes to institutional care — hospitals,
medication, acute crisis intervention.

The Vilomah condition receives almost nothing.

Not because the need is not documented. Because the condition does not fit the medical model. The medical model asks: can we fix this? The Ananta state answers: no. And so the framework moves on.

Evermore. The Echoes Project. The individual Vilomah who writes a book, posts on a web page, makes someone uncomfortable, stands up in any given room and says — I am Vilomah — and refuses to sit back down quietly.

That bell has been ringing since 1950.

It is still ringing.

* * *

You were never invisible.

The world just refused to look.

Now you know.

CHAPTER 9

The Pattern — How Ananta Was Found

It started with a professor.

She was onto something that the clinical world had been circling for decades without naming. She gave us the word Vilomah — Sanskrit, against the natural order — and in doing so she handed every bereaved parent in the English-speaking world something that had been missing from the record since the first inversion ever occurred.

A name.

I followed her pattern. If Sanskrit held the word for what we were — Vilomah, the parent who has outlived a child — then maybe Sanskrit held the word for what we carry. Not the event. Not the inversion. But the state that follows. The thing that conventional therapy has no framework for because conventional therapy was built around the assumption that things resolve.

This does not resolve.

I went looking for the word for that. For the lingering. For the constant that never goes away. For the state of being that exists on good days and bad days and ordinary Tuesday mornings with equal weight — conscious, present, permanent.

Sanskrit. Ananta.

Infinite. Without end.

That is it. That is exactly it.

Not a metaphor. Not a poetic device. A precise, forensic description of the state that every Vilomah enters and never leaves. The death of a child does not have an endpoint. It does not resolve into acceptance. It does not complete itself at stage five and release you back into ordinary life. It becomes a permanent conscious state — present in the background of every moment, every conversation, every room you walk into for the rest of your life.

Professor Holloway gave us Vilomah — the word for what we are.

Sanskrit gave us Ananta — the word for what we carry.

The pattern held.

Vilomah — against the natural order.

Ananta (अनन्त) — infinite, without end.

Two words. Two truths. One record.

This is the fourth law of the Ananta record: *The state of being Vilomah does not end. It is carried consciously, permanently, on good days and bad days and every ordinary day in between. Conventional therapy was not built to hold this. Ananta was.*

The record acknowledges it now.

Now you know.

CHAPTER 10

What Ananta Is

Let me be precise.

Ananta is not a therapy. It is not a grief model. It is not a stage, a framework, a clinical intervention, or a self-help system. It is not something you complete. It is not something you graduate from.

Ananta is a forensic architecture.

It is the permanent, structured acknowledgment that when a child dies, a record is created that does not end. That record is not a wound to be healed. It is not a void to be filled. It is not a burden to be processed away. It is a fact. Permanent. Indexed. True.

The Ananta record has four components.

The Name. Every child who died has a name. The record begins there. Not with the death. Not with the inversion. With the name. Keith Allen Richards. Jon David Wittenburg. Lauren Elizabeth Wittenburg. The name is the first entry in the forensic record and it does not change. It does not fade. It does not become less true with time.

The Life. The record holds the life, not just the death. 9.14 ounces. Two teeth. A head full of hair. & All boy. Thick as thieves. Quiet but always there. The life is the record. The death is only the point at which the record became permanent.

The Inversion. The record names what happened structurally. Not emotionally. Not clinically. Structurally. The natural order inverted. The floor became the ceiling. The timeline that was supposed to move forward stopped and reversed. The Ananta record names this without softening it, without staging it, without asking it to resolve.

The Conscious State. This is what conventional therapy cannot hold and what Ananta was built specifically to acknowledge. The Vilomah does not return to baseline after the inversion. They enter a permanent conscious state in which the absence of the child is present — on good days, bad days, ordinary days — with equal weight. Not as dysfunction. Not as failure to heal. As truth. The Ananta state is the honest description of what it means to carry this baseline for the rest of a life.

That is the full framework. Four components. One record. Permanent.

Conventional therapy asks the Vilomah to move through something that does not move. Ananta asks nothing. It simply holds the record exactly as it is — without judgment, without timeline, without the expectation of resolution.

Professor Holloway gave us Vilomah — the word for what we are.

Sanskrit gave us Ananta — the word for what we carry.

The framework gives us the record — the architecture for holding both truthfully for as long as a life lasts.

This is the fifth final law of the Ananta record:

The record does not ask you to heal. It asks you to be a witness.

* * *

For Keith.

For Jon.

For Lauren.

For the 18.7 million.

The graphite is permanent.

The pencil has no eraser.

Now you know.

A DECLARATION

I need — not want, need — for the world to wake up.

Need is a requirement. Want is a desire. This is a requirement.

I am not asking for money. I am not asking at

all.

I am ensuring that for as long as I am drawing a breath I will be present — to help those who are in need. If that means I write a book, I write a book. If that means I post on a web page, I post on a web page. If that means I make you uncomfortable — then you have something to deal with.

Good.

There is a mountain of people in this world who deserve respect. I did not make those numbers up. I am a part of that tribe.

They never go anywhere.

That is what is actually good about Ananta. It is a blessing.

We wear it on our sleeve not as grief but as witness. To stand in any room at any given moment and say — I am Vilomah — is not a declaration of suffering. It is a declaration of presence. Of love that does not end. Of a record that is permanent. It is standing as proof that they lived. That they are. Present. Always.

The Grief Industry wants the death off the sleeve because it makes other people uncomfortable. Ananta says no. Their presence on your sleeve is the truth. Keith is present. Jon is present. Lauren is present.

Not were.

Are.

They never go anywhere.

That is the blessing.

* * *

I am Vilomah.

I am in Ananta.

I am exactly where I am supposed to be.

— *David Wittenburg, The Witness*

CLOSING

The Witness Statement

There are days when life just moves.

Not good days exactly. Not bad days. Just days when the machinery of living keeps running and you are in it — present, functional, breathing — and the weight is not on the surface. The Ananta state recedes to the background. The record is still there but it is not loud.

And then you remember you did not remember.

That takes my breath away just saying it. The moment you realize that Keith was not in your conscious mind for a stretch of time. That Jon was not in the room of your thoughts for a morning. That Lauren was not in the first thing you felt when you woke up.

And the weight arrives. Not of the death. Of the forgetting.

We do not carry the death of those we love on our sleeve. The world taught us not to. The world built a system specifically designed to move the Vilomah back toward function as quickly as possible — to get the death off the sleeve and back inside where it is manageable and quiet and does not make other people uncomfortable.

Maybe we should carry it on our sleeve.

Not as performance. Not as public grief. But as honest acknowledgment that the Ananta state does not take days off. That on the good days, the ordinary days, the days when life is moving — Keith is still gone. Jon is still gone. Lauren is still gone. And the 18.7 million who are reading this right now, on whatever kind of day this is for them — their child is still gone too.

Growth comes. I understand that. I have lived it. The architecture rebuilds. The floor levels. The days when life moves become more frequent than the days when it does not.

But at what cost.

That is the question the Grief Industry never asks because the Grief Industry is not interested in the cost. It is interested in the outcome. In the functional baseline. In the bereaved person who has successfully processed and returned to ordinary life.

I am not interested in ordinary life.

I am interested in the truth.

The truth is that I was six years old in a hospital in Stuttgart, Arkansas, and I heard the wailing of my grandmother in the background when they spoke of my brother. And that sound — that particular human sound that has no clinical name and no stage and no treatment protocol — that sound is the most honest thing I have ever heard.

That was Ananta before I had the word for it.

A grandmother who knew. Who did not process. Who did not perform. Who simply made the sound that the body makes when the natural order inverts and the language fails and there is nothing left but the truth of what happened.

We should make that sound more.

We should carry it on our sleeve more.

Not because it helps. Not because it heals. But because it is true. And the truth deserves a witness.

I am that witness.

* * *

In the truth I find life — especially

for those who have lived, who I

have loved and still do.

* * *

For Allen Keith Richards. 1963–1968.

For Jon David Wittenburg. 1994–2015.

For Lauren Elizabeth Wittenburg. 1992–2020.

For the 18.7 million who remembered they did not remember today.

The graphite is permanent.

The pencil has no eraser.

Now you know.

ABOUT THIS BOOK

A brother died. A son died. A daughter died.

The English language has no word for what remains.

Sanskrit does.

Vilomah — against the natural order.

Ananta (अनन्त) — infinite, without end.

The permanent, conscious state that every bereaved parent enters and never leaves. Not a stage. Not a diagnosis. Not a condition to be treated and resolved.

A state of being.

18.7 million parents in the United States have outlived a child. Nearly one billion children have died globally since 1950. The world counted the children. Nobody counted the parents.

Ananta is the forensic architecture built for the ones who were never counted. The permanent record that holds the name, the life, the inversion, and the conscious state — without judgment, without timeline, without the expectation of resolution.

This is not a grief manual. There are no stages here. No clinical distance. No roadmap back to ordinary life.

This is the record.

For Keith.

For Jon.

For Lauren.

For the 18.7 million the language forgot.

The graphite is permanent.

The pencil has no eraser.

Now you know.

IF YOU NEED SUPPORT

This book is not therapy. It was never meant to be. But if you are carrying this and you need a hand — not a stage, not a five-step program, a hand — here is where to look.

For Bereaved Parents:

Evermore — evermore.org

National nonprofit dedicated to bereaved parents and families. Data, resources, peer support, and policy advocacy. The most comprehensive bereaved parent resource in the United States.

The Compassionate Friends — compassionatefriends.org *National peer support organization for bereaved parents, grandparents, and siblings. Local chapters in every state.*

Faith's Lodge — faithslodge.org

Retreat center for parents coping with the death of a child. A physical space to reflect, build strength, and connect with other bereaved parents.

Crisis Support:

988 Suicide and Crisis Lifeline — call or text 988

Available 24 hours a day, 7 days a week. If you are in crisis, please call.

Crisis Text Line — text HOME to 741741

Free, 24/7 crisis support via text message.

End of Life Care and Peer Support:

National Alliance for Mental Illness — nami.org | 1-800-950-NAMI

Peer support, education, and advocacy for those affected by mental health conditions including complicated grief.

SC SHARE — sc-share.org

South Carolina state-level peer support advocacy. Connecting those with lived experience to those who need support.

The Echoes Project: thewitnessechoes.com echoesproject.substack.com

Four podcasts built for the 18.7 million. No stages. No platitudes. The truth, weekly.

A note on peer support:

Peer support is not therapy. It is the practice of one person with lived experience walking alongside another. It is the oldest form of support that exists — and for the Vilomah, often the most honest. If you are entering the Ananta state for the first time and you do not know where to turn, find another Vilomah. They will understand what no clinical framework can fully hold.

You are not alone.

You are not broken.

You are Vilomah.

Ananta.

The record holds you.

ABOUT THE AUTHOR

David Wittenburg is a Vilomah — twice. Father of Jon, who died at 21. Father of Lauren, who died at 28. Brother of Keith, who died at four years old in Stuttgart, Arkansas, in 1968.

He is the founder of The Echoes Project, a four-podcast network built for the 18.7 million

bereaved parents in the United States. He is the author of The Witness Series — five books mapping the permanent architecture of catastrophic loss. He is the creator of the Ananta Forensic Record — a forensic
framework for the ones the language forgot.

He is not a therapist or a grief counselor.

He is a witness.

His work is supported by formal study in End of Life Care through USC Upstate and peer support certification in progress through
SC

SHARE. The Ananta Framework is formally documented in the academic record at SSRN: papers.ssrn.com/sol3/papers.cfm?abstract_id=6761738

thewitnessechoes.com ·
anantavilomah.com

Apple Podcasts · Spotify · Substack

David Wittenburg · The Witness · The Echoes Project

ALSO BY

DAVID WITTENBURG

The Witness Series:

Vol. I — The Echoes of Time

Vol. II — Empty Chairs: A Survivor's Story

Vol. III — Vilomah

Vol. IV — Cost

The Echoes Project Podcasts:

The Echoes Project — The 3 AM Inventory

Vilomah: The Witness Archives

The Science of Being: The Kitchen Table

OTG | Off the Grid

www.ingramcontent.com/pod-product-compliance
Lightning Source LLC
LaVergne TN
LVHW010937110826
845149LV00013B/2647
* 9 7 9 8 9 9 5 6 1 3 9 6 1 *